Radiant Obstacles

For Bonnie —

Radiant Obstacles

Poems

LUKE HANKINS

Luke Hankins

Fellow worker in words.

WIPF & STOCK · Eugene, Oregon

7-14-21

RADIANT OBSTACLES
Poems

Wipf & Stock
An Imprint of Wipf and Stock Publishers
199 W. 8th Ave., Suite 3
Eugene, OR 97401

www.wipfandstock.com

PAPERBACK ISBN: 978-1-7252-6208-9
HARDCOVER ISBN: 978-1-7252-6209-6
EBOOK ISBN: 978-1-7252-6210-2

Manufactured in the U.S.A.   03/05/20

Contents

IV

V

Acknowledgments

I'm grateful to the editors of the following publications and programs, in which the listed poems originally appeared:

32 Poems: "Emerald Acres"

American Literary Review: "Wreck"

Archaeopteryx: The Newman Journal of Ideas: "Faith"

The Bellingham Review: "Changeling"

The Blue Mountain Review: "A Voice Out of the Ruins," "Brood X," & "[My haiku about the moon]"

Bluestem: "Dignity and the River"

The Collagist: "Even the River"

The Cortland Review: "Tomorrow My Dad and I Face the Elevator" & "The Dock at the End of the World"

The Curator: "Vapor of Vapors"

Dash Literary Journal: "On Judgment" (winner of the 2016 *Dash Literary Journal* Poetry Contest)

The Equalizer: "That Than Which"

Global Poetry Anthology 2015 (Canada: Signal Editions): "Weather" (shortlisted for the 2015 Montreal International Poetry Competition)

Letters: "The Sculptor"

Levure Litérraire: "Dispatch from the Field to Headquarters" & "Without a Word, Without an Image"

Linebreak: "Beloved"

Modern Literature: "Vow," "The Garden Reaches," & "Wake"

Poetry East: "Spring Prayer"

Porter Gulch Review: "Torn & Tangled"

Presence: A Journal of Catholic Poetry: "Aid" & "A Radiant Obstacle"

Ruminate: "Adam" (finalist for the 2014 Janet B. McCabe Poetry Prize)

ACKNOWLEDGMENTS

St. Katherine Review: "Equal and Opposite," "Meditation," "The Body," & "In the Presence of Beauty"

The Southern Poetry Anthology, Vol. VII: North Carolina (Texas Review Press, 2015): "Two Views" & "Black Mountain, North Carolina"

storySouth: "Divided" (honorable mention in the 2015 North Carolina Writers' Conference Randall Jarrell Poetry Competition)

Town Creek Poetry: "Tree Rings" & "A Way of Knowing"

The Turnip Truck(s): "Midnight Orchard"

TXTOBJX: "Coming To" & "Night Garden"

The World Is Charged: Poetic Engagements with Gerard Manley Hopkins (Clemson University Press & Liverpool University Press, 2016): "All Fall Long"

"Equal and Opposite" was reprinted in *The Poet's Quest for God* (Eyewear Publishing, UK, 2016).

"The Way They Loved Each Other" was featured both on air on and on the blog of the American Public Media radio program "On Being" (www.being.publicradio.org).

The world is the closed door. It is a barrier.
And at the same time it is the way through.

—SIMONE WEIL

A VOICE OUT OF THE RUINS

Nostalgia for a place I've never been. Remembered intimacy with a person I've never known. A voice out of the ruins of Eden, calling me back, not into Eden, but into what is possible there, where Eden once stood, in the ruins.

I

VOW

Beauty brings copies of itself into being.
    —ELAINE SCARRY

I have made no vow of undying love

                      except to moments like this one,
as water flames out, flung

              from the dog bowl, over the hydrangea leaves—
a sunlit wing extended and sparkling

                  for a bare moment
before it collapses into the earth—

              the very Icarus of beauty.

Why is it so tempting

           to say the love of a thing
is dependent on its loss?

            Is this the temptation into which God fell
when She made these ants

             crawling across my open book,
intricate mechanisms

           that will live a few weeks?

How can God bear to bring so much into being

                  in Her zeal to create—
saying *It is good, It is good*

           at each genesis—
only to let it all so quickly die?

     Beauty brings copies of itself into being says the philosopher.

So the queen ant produces brood after brood,

4

                sends her grotesque offspring,

each animate replica,

          into the world to work before succumbing

to the common fate of every spark.

So the artist tries to record the moment water

                was fanned in air and lit

like the appendage of a transparent bird

           hovering over the hydrangea leaves.

So a mosquito bites a stray dog

            and heartworm larvae enter its bloodstream,

settle and grow in its heart

          before sending their own larvae into the blood

to be transported

        through a mosquito to the next host.

      So *beauty brings*

           copies of itself

             into being.

And who are we to say

        the water in flight,

            the ant,

               the artist,

the work of art,

      the mosquito,

          the dog,

            and the heartworms

are not equally beautiful to God,

who experiences
the birth and life and death
of each being and event simultaneously?

Does She suffer as She rejoices?
Is She consoled
by the successive generations of Her creation?

I could not presume to know the Maker's mind,
but I know something of my own—
I could not bear
to make such magnificent and fleeting things.

But being here,
having been brought, briefly, into being,
I gather in my mind the moments I glimpse a marvelous life
or witness a startling arrangement of matter.

Though these things all pass away, I vow
to harbor them until,
like heartworms,
they bring so many copies of themselves into being
I die of it.

THE GARDEN REACHES

The most remarkable thing has happened—

I exist, and you,
                    reading this.

The clack of beak on beak
                            and skull on skull
as hummingbirds divebomb one another
                                        in the garden reaches
my ears and that sound exists
        and what it testifies to,
                        too, is equally real.

Let the hibiscus nod its assent
                        as the hummingbird drinks
from the blossom
                for which it has so viciously fought.

        Let beak meet beak and not blank air
                                    when the buzzing birds
defend their feeding grounds,
                    let tongue find nectar
        where red invited the bird to gorge.

    Step into the garden.
                        Touch the flower, trembling in the wake.
        Touch this word for *flower*,
                            signaling to you
    from across the page.

            Is there any nectar there?

This word in your hands,

                    accosting your eye,

touch it.

          This word.

                And *this*.

      Can you?

THE SCULPTOR

Here again in conflict—

                a block of stone—

the task:

        to make a permanence

                fitting tribute

to what dissipates—

        a hand,

            a gaze,

a gesture

      affixed

        in broken stone.

What are we

        and by whose hand?

The inverse

      of what I create,

I am a temporary likeness,

          a fading image

of something eternal,

        making

           until I am undone.

KEATS

What years I've had have been spent
in an attempt to form something symmetrical,
coherent, and yet as uncertain
as a curtain of fog hanging shapely
about a mountain's waist. All I've wanted
was to give my thoughts a shape

that resembles something in this world,
to describe without providing false assurances.
There is a limit to what we can know,
and our work must embody
rather than defy that limitation.
I always knew I would not endure

long in this world, and the consumptive
death I face is all too fitting
for a life dedicated to denying assurance.
If I could have chosen, I would not have been
born. My name—and my poems, too—are writ
in water. Perhaps it would have better served

to have left the water undisturbed.

MERCY KILLS

It was a two mercy kills day.

First: a snake. I stepped into the road
to move it into the woods
but a car came hurtling toward us and I
watched the tires bludgeon
the snake. It was still moving.
I found a heavy stone. Wincing,
I slammed it down,
and had to several times.

Second: a possum. It flashed
into my headlights
and there was no time
to stop before I felt the sickening bump.
I turned the car around to make certain
it was dead. It wasn't. It was writhing—
no, I'd have to say *roiling*,
like a serpent. I ran it over again,
aiming for its head; reversed
the car. Again.

My hands felt dirty the rest of the night.
More than once I woke and scrubbed them,
stupid as it sounds.

To comfort me, some might
call me merciful.
Don't call me merciful.

Call me mercy's executioner.

DIVIDED

The two parts
            of the decapitated copperhead
both live on—or seem to—
                for minutes after the severing.
The body wrings itself,
               the mouth gapes on open air,
and then the blind tail writhes into
                  the open mouth,
which bites down savagely
               on its former self.
The body recoils and rolls in a vain attempt
                     to dislodge the teeth
that once fed it,
          a house divided
               against itself—
by shovel blade divided.

I will put enmity between you . . . .
               He will crush your head,
and you will strike his heel.

          How greatly fallen
this mighty house
         of bone, organ, muscle, and fang,

warred on by a man afraid of poison.
                What triumph does he feel
in living to see
        the serpent biting its own heel?

EMERALD ACRES

Rough field of sunglaze
                  on muting glass,
each pane half opaque
                and cradling light,
twenty acres of greenhouse glowing
                        in the sun, abandoned now
a year or more,
              an angular architecture
                        neither green
nor housing anything,
                though light takes up residence
on bright days or overcast,
                  on moonlit nights or star-pricked.
An armor
           for the humid air,
      full of gaps
                where kids have stoned out the panes.

No protection,
           but an appearance.
Twenty acres of ruin,
           a slowly failing house
—but a house nonetheless—
             for an idea about beauty.

II

ADAM

CF. HEBREW, "ADAMAH" ("EARTH"; "GROUND")

We're losing him. I sat him down
    for a picture yesterday,
and he wouldn't smile. All he'd say
    was *My leaves are gone.*
He sighed like the winter wind was in his lungs.
    When we had the photo developed I saw
a body of branches, a head of brush.
    He wrote *Son of Earth*
        on the reverse.
From somewhere deep inside him came a *caw.*

    His teacher called me just last week
        to tell me what he'd done
at recess—cornered a girl, touched her cheek,
    said *Flesh of my flesh, bone of my bone* . . . .
        She recoiled as if she'd been struck,
and people say she's starting to turn odd—
        the veins that once were tucked
        unseen beneath her skin
           now look like thin
branches, and she smells of sod.

    I'm afraid he won't last long.
He's taken to standing on the lawn
        for hours at a time,
swaying there, or lying silent
in leaf-piles. He doesn't seem to mind
        what's happening. He's quiet,
mostly, though he shakes with sighs
        and shivers now and then.
    I just wish he'd touch me so I
        too could follow him.

WEATHER

Out in the gusty night every hinged
thing works: the pool-gate clacks, the shed door
swings back and forth. Broken shutters
fall halfway off their windowframes. The winds
pick up a disarray and scatter it again.
The weather comes at us through the dark, dragging
a storm like a busted toy. Unconcerned, cracking
everything it passes with its wheelless wagon,
the weather makes itself at home. But it's fine
with me. It bullies me inside and I forget
the repairs I'll have to make tomorrow—more urgent
is my daughter squeezing her hand into mine.
More pressing than the wild play outside
is this work, calming a child who would have cried.

EVEN THE RIVER

In a constant murmur of leaves and branches
the mountains have been speaking to me
about how you left them, cardinals
flashing in and out of branches
signaling in red semaphore their grief
at your departure. All of nature
seems to address and blame me.
I walk around holding out my hands,
palms upturned, in a gesture
of bewilderment and surrender,
suggesting my innocence
but also my willingness to hold
the guilt that finds no other place to rest.
I go out at midnight to comfort the river
near the tracks where the trains pass
in a slow, unrelenting fury all night,
the spark of metal on metal
winding through the dark,
blaring their enormous questions
that I don't know how to answer.
And even the river resists my touch,
like a small child who continues
to feel slighted
no matter how long
her father sits by her bed
stroking her hair and singing.

"DON'T GO IN THERE"

FOR MOM AND KEITH AND MEGAN

My mom and I were watching a movie once,
and someone was dying of tuberculosis.
His brother went in to hold him as he struggled for breath.
Being who I am, I told the character on screen,
"Don't go in there . . . " Mom said, "They didn't know about germs then.
But I'd go in anyway." And she would have—she would
do it for me, for anyone she loved.
Do you know what I would do?
I don't. I'd probably be stuck hesitating
at the locked door of my self-love.
Once, in my simultaneous loss of faith and fear of hell,
a friend told me that he would take
all of my despair and misery
upon himself, if he could, if he could.
And there was not the least shade of insincerity in his voice.
I am a coward and nothing like him. That heroic love stuns me.
Another friend told me
in the midst of my very real fear of eternal damnation
that she would take God's wrath for me.
That would be impossible—but her kind of love
is also impossible, and yet is real, was right there
looking at me, clear-eyed and unflinching.
So who's to say that she hasn't actually taken
God's wrath for me, and God turned it into an embrace
because she offered herself up like Jesus himself?
I don't know if Jesus is who I used to think he was,
but I know what I saw right there in front of me,
and I know the impossible words I heard.
I don't think I deserve hell, but I know for certain
that I don't deserve the kind of love Megan revealed to me,
or that Keith calmly placed at my feet.

I don't deserve my mom coming into my tubercular deathbed, as she most assuredly and unhesitatingly would.

TOMORROW MY DAD AND I FACE THE ELEVATOR

Tomorrow my dad and I face the elevator
at the BB&T building, bound
for the 11th floor, on business.
That may not sound like much.
But for a man and his son
who share the same intense phobias,
it's terrifying. Because I know
what it means for him to face those
clamping doors, that closed cage of a room,
I won't let him go alone. It's the cage
of the mind in front of us. That's the fear—
the mind breaking down between floors,
the door refusing to open. To tell the truth,
it doesn't necessarily help to have someone else there,
even him for me or me for him.
But I will go with him, even if all I can do
as our separate minds lock down
in panic is pound steadily on my wall
next to his wall to let him faintly hear
I know. I know. I know. I know.

WISHING WELL

A man plays guitar and sings at the mic
for what passes as a crowd on a Tuesday night,
coming up on midnight, and the bartender makes
a round, leaving the bar to pick up empty glasses,
laughing with a couple here and there, and touching
lonely men lightly on the shoulder as she passes,
with an unassailable reserve, but also a kind
of tenderness, saying a word or only grinning briefly
as she moves among her little congregation,
holding back the emotion that has built
over months and years of seeing these regulars
come in so often alone, nodding silently
to acknowledge one another, but rarely speaking,
heads in their cups or raised to the screen,
or glancing at her behind the bar,
unattainable yet always near.
She loves them, and they know it when she passes
her eyes over them, or touches them almost
imperceptibly as she gathers glasses, and it is the look
of a mother, the weight of a partner
dancing with them sometime in the past.
What's unsaid can't be broken. And so the men stumble
one by one to the bathroom, making their incoherent wishes
without insisting, without demanding anything of God,
relishing secretly their exquisite loneliness,
standing at the urinal pissing on the pennies and dimes
someone tossed there who knows when, for who knows why.

DIGNITY AND THE RIVER

The torrents of rain have passed, but the river
in the back yard boils up with mud
and sloshes back and forth. Does it remember
the now-passed downpour the way a man would
remember, watching such a river, the power
of a force too much for him to bear without
it showing as a turmoil—now he'll bow (Or
is it less voluntary?) in a gale-force, wait it out
bent and puny, as unmanly as a reed;
now he'll spring up shaking at what's passed—
a turmoil in his words and actions, his need
for pity and his need for love fast
swelling the banks of his prodigious dignity?
Dignity—from the Latin for what is *fitting*.
But nothing fits anymore. You see,
it's a fit of weather that fills him to splitting.

THE DOCK AT THE END OF THE WORLD

When you're sad, we'll go walking through the fog
until we find the dock at the end of the world
where we can peer into the vacuum of space
and dance a silent waltz to no music,
making our own time,
left-two-three toward the shore,
right-two-three toward the nearest star.

~

The fog has cleared now
and we're standing in the cold breeze
listening to the patter of snow flurries on our coats.
The lampposts behind us shed an eerie light
over the dock at the end of the world,
casting our shadows halfway across the water.
We reach up
and the hands of our shadows
touch the far shore.

A VALEDICTION FORBIDDING NOTHING

AFTER DONNE

They need not know our love, but let
them know it, anyway. If we
must part, then let them not forget
that we are parting painfully.

We've often told them that our love
is heavenly and spirit-born,
that it's *coming in from above,*
like in that '70s song. Honey, mourn

for me, if I have to leave, because
that's all a load of shit. Your body
is important to me—babe, it does
what makes you you. We may well be

gold pounded to a sheet as thin
as air, almost, when we have
to separate—but don't forget the din
the hammer makes. We may be halves

of a metal compass, like the ones
we used to use in geometry—
but we might as well admit, unlike Donne's,
our compass hinge is rather rusty,

not being made of gold, and shrieks
an awful squeal as it's wrenched
apart. Our souls commune, yours speaks
to mine—but the body's where the deal is cinched.

...ING

...ith all the hearts a worm has,
...n concert. With all the eyes
...as, I relish you. No dog
...ur scent as I do, no cat the heat
...ap. When you let me hold you,
you are the eucalyptus and I the koala clinging.
This bat will suck the nectar from you
and hang in the dark of your mind.
Tusk of narwhal, rooster's spur,
tongue of aardvark, marmot's fur.
When this animal's passion passes,
watch me turn into another one.

III

SIGNAL

Across the field a woman signals to another woman

with a gesture unintelligible to me as a hieroglyph.

Dusk, and the field appears limitless and restive as the sea.

This seems like a place I have memories of, but only seems that way.

These women, I'd guess, do have memories of this place—

here something began or ended for them.

I've come here to pray, but find myself only trembling.

And now with their hands they're searching close to the ground

like blind women might.

MIDNIGHT ORCHARD

In the fog
        an eye
glowing

       In the eye
a glowing
      fog

   ~

Lobs of fruit depend
             groundward
upon
      apple trees

Apple trees
       depend upon
lobs
         of groundward
     fruit

   ~

designs, pendant—
         dependent signs

   ~

The moon like an eye
like the fruit like the moon

An eye like the fruit
like the moon like an eye

The fruit like the moon
like an eye like the fruit

TREE RINGS

Here is a history that does not concern you,
a making apart
                    without
the imposition of form, a shapely
patient expansion, except not
patient because it is mindless.
But you cannot help regarding
the sawn trunk allegorically
(devoted becoming, then the desolate
crash through other limbs).
Do we not also expand ourselves
and thus can speak of the slow
sorrow of the trees even though
we know they are not sad,
not slow, except in
our perceiving? It is enough
to perceive a thing for it to bear
the force of truth.
                    So,
the hillside stands of trees driving
minutely upward through mindless
centuries. Their jagged symmetries
unerringly perpetuate
and the soft new leaves,
the supple branches giving way
to the wind, seem just like us
though they are not.

A WAY OF KNOWING

I.

Dawn

The stream lifts from itself in the early light,
hanging in a hammock of bare branches.
It does not move away, it does not slide
east or west, does not break
the skeletal banks of branches overarching
the stream. A leaf sways in place on a spider web
like a bone-dry fish hovering in the current
of the risen line of fog which is the stream's
second self. This the transient knowledge.

II.

Day

All without knowledge is itself in the bright cool
and works steadily at its business like the roots
of trees at the soil, working up through
their bodies what they glean and gathering
as they grow a solid stance for their upsprung
trunks and branches but unknowing those
second selves as they work and the wind
bows the trees and the roots do not know
their work is the buttress for their selves above.

III.

Moonlight

Fog the mountain's second self
risen from the mountain and in it I
am and my second self is and as the mountain
of mountain I of I am aware—as the body
is known to me so incompletely I am
aware of my second self sporadically
that second body within and throughout
risen now aware I of I in the mountain
as much as on it in the fog of.

MEDITATION

I'm like the reflection of snow in a lake
moving upward (or so it appears)
to meet the snow itself—what You are—
as it falls and fills the lake.

I'm not even the lake.
I'm just what light does on its surface—
the sky-depth of that
and the two-dimensionality.

When we touch, it is the touch of a Thing
to an idea. I am obliterated, but reborn
in Your melting, an image of what is above me
in what is beyond me.

You are. Therefore, in a small way, I am.

[MY HAIKU ABOUT THE MOON]

My haiku about the moon
is not quite right,
but the moon is right.

TWO VIEWS

I.

Summer night descending
on the thick woods.
No green remaining,
no trees with green fingers
or yellow broken ones.
None present themselves,
their spiderweb lace
and beaded moss.
We are ill equipped
to dream a forest into being.
Only, here and there, an old breeze
tottering through the limbs
catches matter
in the nonwoods.

II.

Summer morning rising
on the sparse woods.
Green returns,
trees with green fingers
and yellow broken ones.
They present themselves,
their spiderweb lace
and beaded moss.
We are well equipped
to dream a forest into being.
Only, here and there, a fresh breeze
coursing through the limbs
touches nothing
in the nonwoods.

COMING TO

I came to
what had been
and there
it was before
me I came
to what had
not been and I
ceased to be

I came before
it was there
and there it
was before me
I came to
what had been
before me
and it ceased

to be I
came to
and there it was
before I ceased
to be what had
and not been
before I
came before it

THE NIGHT GARDEN

I am the waterer of the night garden.
I can hardly see.
I water what I remember
being there.

ALL FALL LONG

I can feel fall
and a falling feeling—
feeling The Fall
and what was fallen from
in the cool air—
both foreign and familiar.
And the feeling comes on,
falling through me, and rising,
rousing me, awe-full all fall long.

BLACK MOUNTAIN, NORTH CAROLINA

A chill, bright, breeze-chased day in December—
a clearing after days of dampness,
and I have never seen clouds quite like this—
not hovering in the broad blueness of the sky,
but only hugging the mountains,
as if someone had snapped a sheet like a whip
in the air above them, and brought it down,
dragging its weight across the contours
of the Blue Ridge, or as if the expansive hand
of Winter itself, miles-wide, had grasped the ridgeline
to pull itself forward over the land.

BROOD X

ASHEVILLE, NORTH CAROLINA, 2008

And suddenly this spring the whirring of a vast machinery
in the trees, an unseen ubiquity of sound
that indicates aliens to children and the mad.
But the truth is, risen from the ground
after seventeen years as nymphs, these
are the opposite of aliens, come out of the earth
itself to whirr among the boughs, to mate
and let their offspring fall into familiar soil.

APRIL

The pear trees have bloomed
and the air is full of their
sweet, sexual scent.

How to exit my body
yet take the body with me?

April evening air,
cool after a warm day—
I feel I should grow.

Green-tongued poplar bud, I know
it wasn't easy, I know.

THEIR BEAUTIFUL FISTS

I know the blossoming trees are not shaking their beautiful fists at me.
But if you ask me how I feel, I'll say that they're shaking their beautiful fists at me.

IN THE PRESENCE OF BEAUTY

I have known the same
abject misery you have
in the presence of beauty.
It is not the kind
of beauty that elevates
you by association,
because there is no
associating with it. It is
utterly beyond you.
And you go searching
for a much lesser beauty.
It might have been better
to have never encountered it.
That beauty
I cannot do without.

IN THE WOODS

I feel so far from the meaning of the earth.
It is silent. It lives but does not speak.
I will not say that it *should* speak,
only that I want it to
and—no matter how I chide myself—
I wait, listening.

IV

WAKE

The universe begins to look more like a great thought than a great machine.

—Sir James Jeans

Then, dear Lord, what so troubles your dreams?

Continents rise magnificently from the sea

                            and grow green, seethe

with plants and animals—

              but, Lord, they age and decay,

disembowel or swallow whole to digest slowly,

    or plant their eggs in one another's flesh

                       in this dream from which I pray

        You'll wake.

      My childhood friend was born with holes in his heart

and died at 30, afraid, trembling.

            Trembling, Lord.

    (Are You trembling in your sleep?

                Wake.)

      I stood by his open grave prettified with Astroturf.

    70 people died at a funeral in Mozambique yesterday

        by drinking beer contaminated with crocodile poison.

    And crocodiles are poisoned

               because they were born with teeth,

      and hungry, and strong.

A man crying *I can't breathe I can't breathe I can't breathe*
  provokes not the slightest adjustment
                                    of the policeman's grip
            and he drowns in broad air.

        Why these tortured thoughts?

Because we are so in need of comforting, I long to comfort You.

    Wake into a better state of mind,
                            into whatever light
        warms the world in which You sleep.

Do not let your heart be troubled,
                        and cease to trouble ours.

        Wake.

            Undream us.

WRECK

Walking past a telephone pole struck by a car,
I see the pole has been righted,
the wires repaired. I drove by earlier today
as firemen strapped the driver's head
to a spinal board. Plastic and fiberglass detritus
is still scattered on the ground, easily overlooked
testimony of the sudden appearance

                            of an impediment
in the path of the texting driver, perhaps looking up
from his phone just in time to imagine
what was about to happen to him,
what he was about to feel.

                  But, as in any epiphany,
that object did not *appear*, much less
suddenly, and was only experienced
as having done so.

                Blind or distracted soul,
what are you careening toward, and what
already waits to appear

              to you
with bone-shattering suddenness, and awaits
not only what damage it will do,
but what damage it will receive,

                      tilting and splintered
against your headlong and heedless embrace?

THE WAY THEY LOVED EACH OTHER

JULY 14, 2011

What to be more astonished at:
my calm as the fist made contact
and I saw a flash of white
and the world went silent
as if I had stepped out of it
momentarily, only to be brought back
with a rush of sound and visible objects—
the way I asked them to help me
find my glasses, expecting them
(even as they taunted me,
even though they had just assaulted me)
to feel underneath the violent tribal urge
the obligations of empathy—
the way even as one of them found my glasses
and smashed them again on the ground
I refused to believe that was really
what he wanted to do—the way
they loved each other
in the most primitive manner,
but loved each other nonetheless,
despite feeling the need to punish a "faggot"
who did not dress like them, *because*
he did not dress like them—
the way tears and nausea overwhelmed me
nightlong much more than had the blow itself—
the way such small suffering can feel
unbearable—the way no strength is found
for what seems to have no explanation,
a troubled mind more harmful
to the body than fractured bones.

THAT THAN WHICH

> And assuredly that, than which nothing greater can be conceived,
> cannot exist in the understanding alone.
>
> God is whatever it is better to be than not to be.
>
> —ANSELM OF CANTERBURY

nothing that can be
conceived greater than

which can be
nothing

nothing can be
greater than that
conceived

that which can
be nothing

can nothing
be greater

be conceived
greater nothing

~

it is better to be than not to be

whatever

it is not

not better
than to be

50

whatever is better
than not to be
it is

whatever it is
to be

~

can whatever is greater
be conceived
to not be

nothing better
than to be conceived
not to be

which is it

whatever
can be
it can not

to be is nothing greater
than to be conceived

is it
better to be
than not to be

to be conceived
is nothing

nothing
can be conceived

A RADIANT OBSTACLE

> Why is there something rather than nothing?
> —GOTTFRIED WILHELM VON LEIBNIZ

Leibniz's question would have made
Zeno giddy—the ancient Greek
whose mathematical paradoxes
disproved motion and discredited math:
Any distance between points A and B
can be divided innumerable times,
therefore requiring an infinite amount
of time to cross.
          For millennia
his proofs remained unshakeable,
lingering in the recesses of the minds
of mathematicians and philosophers,
casting doubt on the unadulterated
language of numbers and reason.

Steiner called the Question of Being
a radiant obstacle in the path of the obvious.
But Zeno, not content with mere obstacles,
simply made movement down the path
—and the path itself—impossible.
See the proofs that make the obvious alien.
See reason's vacuum, the black hole of logic,
out of which, Zeno knew,

                an impossible path radiates.

EQUAL AND OPPOSITE

Looking at the sky, the word *sky*
comes to mind. The word has a referent—
the sky itself—but the sky itself
has no referent. To live in language
is to anticipate metaphor,
but in this moment I sense the void
upon which, all these years, I have built
my house of words.
Only come with me
to the precipice where I peer in terror,
I pray, grasping at words
that offer no resistance
like feathers snatched from the air,
like ropes not tied to anything.
I plunge through the world
that is no language
praying (in my language)
to the absent Referent,
the force equal and opposite
to the void, the grip that can
(I pray) suspend my fall
so that I might hang
in what the sky means.

WITHOUT A WORD, WITHOUT AN IMAGE

How does one hold it in the mind? An idea without words. It is there after the words, in the mind without even a trace of an image. An idea or a question, bodiless and wordless, after the words which arose from it in the first place. How does one go on feeling it without a word, without an image?

You are doing it now. If these words ended here, if all the words in your own mind fell away, it would still be there. The very question of how one holds a question in the mind—you are holding that in your mind and still would be if you ceased to think it in words.

It is neither words nor images. It is pure abstraction, and any words that come arose from it. You hold it in the mind, that feeling, that idea, that question. The question came before the words that pose it. This is the soul, holding it. Even now, it is there without a word, without an image.

FAITH

*DEDICATED TO HAROLD CAMPING, AFTER HIS
FINAL FAILED PROPHECY*

Now he will have to face
the breathing machine,
the morphine, the ordinary
death, the humiliation
of having thought himself
bestowed a rare place
in the ecclesiastical annals,
a soul privileged
to see the Lord
returning on the clouds,
to meet him in the air.
At 89, he at last
encounters his mortality
and trembles, wondering if
his faith, too, will prove mortal.
"Sue," he says to his daughter
on the phone as the hour
of his rapture passes,
"I'm a little bewildered."

SPRING PRAYER

Allow me
to accept
this April
afternoon's
sunlight,
warm on
my arm,
that simple
delight,
for what
it is—
pleasure
without
price.

Let me
release
my grip
on guilt
for just
this little
while.
I would
not dim
this bright
touch by
hiding in
the shade of
my heart.

Let spring
arrive

here, too.
May I
forget to
not bloom.
And forgive
my constant
requests for
forgiveness,
even now
tainting this—
ah, warm!—
moment.

THE RIGHT WAY

Dietrich Bonhoeffer wrote in a letter from prison,
The transcendence of epistemological theory
has nothing to do with the transcendence of God.
Which, given, is an epistemological theory all its own . . . .
But the sentiment is right. It feels right to say that sentence.
And so I say it over and over, and I write it again and again.
He also says that *God's "beyond" is not the beyond*
of our cognitive faculties. Hmm. I can't
technically agree with either statement,
as they seem to arise out of the very processes
they're attempting to discount. It involves a logical fallacy
for which I'm sure logicians have a name.
But I do say *yes* to these statements.
I do memorize and repeat them.
Dear Bonhoeffer, I don't agree, but I feel you, man.
It's strange—I could almost be talking to myself.
Heaven nowhere more possible than in the depths of hell,
I write. *God as reason beyond reason.*
Dear Me, I feel you, man. I think
you're wrong, but wrong in the right way.

BELOVED

Drunk and faltering
in my midnight chair,
someone gripped me
by the hair and raised my head.
I saw St. Theresa of Avila,
with St. John of the Cross and Rumi
by her side, arm in arm.
And then through the door behind them
came Rabia Al-Basri and Bashō,
all with garish, wine-drenched smiles,
blood-purple lips.
They asked me, "What are you doing?"
and I said "No, what are *you* doing?"
They said, "We are drunk on the wine of the beloved."
I said, "I am drunk but have no beloved."
St. Theresa pulled my hair harder
and said, "Oh, yes you do!"—
and smothered me
with her wine-soured mouth.

ON JUDGMENT

In canine mythology
Sisyphus is the most blessèd of all,
granted an eternal game of fetch.

VAPOR OF VAPORS

I pass by the running river
like a mist moving across the bank
into sunlight.
Vanity of vanities,
we all recognize from the King James,
but that's a rather invasive translation
of what the Hebrew literally says—
Vapor of vapors, all is vapor.
It's an observation—something
we all notice to varying degrees,
and it's a lament—something
we're not at all happy about.
So how is it that when we hear it
we find it beautiful?

CLAUSTROPHOBIA

When even wide blue sky
and white clouds scattered far
incite claustrophobia—
patience, patience.

Soon, night.

You will see clear
through the lightyears.

TORN & TANGLED

> ...I am small,
> but have, as well, too many tentacles
> that grope in the different-being Being.
>
> —M. Vasalis, "Simultaneity"
> (trans. Fred Lessing and David Young)

I've made the mistake
of trying to grasp each strand
of the world's complexity.
The world is too great.
My mind has torn & tangled.
I cannot travel.
I cannot leave anymore
my little habitat
or I will unravel
& tear asunder.
Perhaps Dickinson's mind
was great enough to meet the world—
The Brain is deeper than the sea –
For – hold them – Blue to Blue –
The one the other will absorb –
As Sponges – Buckets do –
—and yet how often did she leave
her hermitage, and stray how far?
I set my sails in a gale.
They have shredded
and I've rowed back to harbor.
I don't think I'll ever again be willing
to raise anchor.

DISPATCH FROM THE FIELD TO HEADQUARTERS

It appears that a mistake has been made.
We are currently stationed in existence.
To be precise, at a point
in evolutionary history
when the human mind
can become overly absorbed
in the quest for meaning
and in the fear of death.
I repeat: A mistake has been made.
It is hard to carry out our mission,
with these metaphysical preoccupations.
Nor can we agree on what our mission is.
Some of us have clearly been misassigned.
Many of us. Perhaps all.
There was no warning.
And I hardly need remind you
that we didn't volunteer—
we were drafted.

AID

The aid I received was
that no one came to my aid.
God in Her power took on powerlessness
particularly in response to my need.
The Doer did nothing.
The Speaker was silent.
The Giver held on to what She had.
How hard that must have been
for Her for whom no difficulty exists!
Try not to resent that
and try not to love Her for it.

CRUCIFIX

Christ hangs from his wrists,
arms fully extended and useless, his full weight
sagging on the nails.

Imagine the gravity of that pendant
on your neck—the moment
when God can no longer pull himself up for a breath,

when the fluid filling his pericardium and pleura
at last smothers him.
But I wear no necklace anymore.

Of all things I've lost
along with my faith, I'll miss most
the ability to pity God.

THIS IS DESPAIR

Was asked:

> *If you could go back in time*
> *and kill any one person,*
> *who would it be?*

Responded:

> *Eve.*

> *Before the kids.*

I SAID TO GOD

I said to God, *Let's make a deal.*
When You take my life,
no anguished anticipation, no long pain,
no fear of dying, no fear of hell—
just peace, satisfaction, relief, a quiet
falling asleep. And—What can I do in return?
Anything You ask. But I think maybe
You owe me as much as I've asked anyway,
having made me, having given me
no choice in the matter . . .

You don't like mortality, God said.
I don't like it at all, I said, *to put it lightly.*
God said, *Do you imagine there's no reason?*
I felt small and dumb, so I didn't speak.
Here's our deal, God said. *I will not deprive you*
of your anguish or your pain or your fear—
least of all, your death.
And you will become
what you cannot otherwise be.

Your deal is hard, I said. *Is it worth it?*
And I grew small and quiet,
waiting in the silence.

EXPERIENCE

I said to myself, *Don't we fear death*
for more reason than one?
There is the fear of the thing itself,
the moment or the hour of it,
the days leading up to it.
There is the fear of what may come.
And there is the fear of nothingness—
the fear that concerns me right now—
the fear of ceasing to be.
I laughed at myself, but kindly,
not wanting to hurt my own feelings
for being such a worrier,
and I said in response,
It's not as if you've never not been before!
Did you care one bit
about not being
then, when you weren't?

URGE

FOR MAURICE

That boredom is the impetus to act
is so hard to remember
in the moment of ennui.
I know someone who says he's never bored.
But God gave the rest of us
boredom so we would seek Her.

Oh God, I've come to the end of desire.
There lives the dearest freshness deep down things—
so Your servant says.
But I've lost the power
to sense it.

This disappearance of desire
feels eternal.

But, then,
the disappearance itself
creates an urge.

ENTERPRISE

I can no longer pray without thinking what a show
I'm making of praying.

I kneel, and in my mind I see myself kneeling.

Congratulations, you scoundrel.

You'd better go write a poem about it.

CONFESSION

I'm trying to feel guilty enough
to feel better about myself.

ɪ the mirror,
if. Prise your eyes
glaze of glass
direction is reversed.
ing forward, one is looking behind.
ɪɪ se my left hand, I see my right rise.
The mind gets lost in that altered world,
forgetting what has changed,
remembering only what has not—
up remains up,
and down, down.

THE BODY

If I tell myself in my mind
to forget the body, the body becomes
increasingly present to the mind.
But if I begin to dance, the body falls away
through its own sensations.

The inscription on the entryway
of the Basilica Saint-Denis in Paris reads,
*The dull mind rises to truth through that which is material
and, in seeing this light, is resurrected from its former submersion.*

The body in motion is a cathedral.

PRAISE

When the mind cannot, the body still knows how to praise.
In my room at night I dance before God,
unthinking, at last.
She makes my mind go quiet,
She makes my body dance.

EX NIHILO

A thousand years are as a day with the Lord
and a day is as a thousand years.
For me, it only works one way at a time.
There was a year in which a day
was as a week, a week
was as a month, a month
was as a year. But now
let my speech about that
measure only seconds.
A year of despair slowly began
to change, in fits and spurts,
fear now abating, now reasserting
a grip that could not be gainsaid.
The pain that can be named
is not the true pain.
But blessèd be that agony.
A different way of being
has been revealed to me.
Is it God? Is it the Tao?
Search me and know me, oh God.
Try me and know my heart
and see if there be any grievous way
in me, and lead me in the everlasting Tao.
I sink into emptiness until I begin
to feel the divinity of the nothing.
Out of nothingness
a new life.
I cannot say how.

Notes

"Keats"   The epitaph John Keats chose for his tomb is "Here lies one whose name was writ in water."

"April"   This poem is a collaborative renga, co-written with Rachel Shopper.

"Faith"   Harold Camping was a preacher who claimed to have discovered a means of predicting the *rapture*—the future event, in fundamentalist Christian belief, in which all Christians will disappear from earth and be taken directly to heaven, followed by the *tribulation*, a period of suffering for those left on earth before the final judgment at the throne of God. Camping made three predictions over the course of his life, later claiming that he had "miscalculated" following the failure of each prophecy except the last, after which he made no public comments. He ran a radio program and had a large following. Many of his followers quit their jobs and sold their possessions in anticipation of his final prophecy, a predicted rapture in 2011. His daughter reported in an interview that after his final prediction failed, he said to her on the phone, "I'm a little bewildered that it didn't happen" (*Los Angeles Times*).

"The Body"   The text inscribed on the entryway of the Basilica Saint-Denis, Paris was written by the 12th-century abbot Suger.

About the Author

Luke Hankins is the author of the poetry collection *Weak Devotions* as well as a collection of essays, *The Work of Creation: Selected Prose*. A book of his translations from the French of Stella Vinitchi Radulescu, *A Cry in the Snow & Other Poems*, was released by Seagull Books in 2019. Hankins is also the editor of *Poems of Devotion: An Anthology of Recent Poets* and is the founder and editor of Orison Books, a non-profit literary press focused on the life of the spirit from a broad and inclusive range of perspectives.